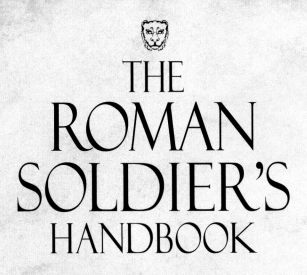

THE ROMAN SOLDIER'S HANDBOOK

Lesley Sims

Designed & illustrated
by Ian McNee

Military expert: Dr. Boris Rankov

A survival guide for the raw recruit

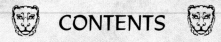 CONTENTS

With thanks to the Ermine Street Guard,
a society dedicated to researching the Roman Army,
for providing the commands on page 23.

First published in 2004 by Usborne Publishing Ltd., Usborne House,
83-85 Saffron Hill, London EC1N 8RT, England. www.usborne.com
Copyright © 2004 Usborne Publishing Ltd.

CHAPTER 1

GETTING STARTED

Welcome, legionary, to the proudest, most professional army in the Western World. It's thanks to the army that our empire is the size it is. You've a tough life ahead but you'll make good friends, travel the world and be rewarded for your efforts with money and land when you retire. (Assuming you make it that far. Just a little army joke to start things off.)

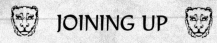

If this book belongs to someone else and you're reading it to see whether army life is for you, check the list of requirements below.

You must:

I. BE AT LEAST 1.75M (5'7") TALL

You'll be measured in bare feet, so don't think you can bring trick shoes.

II. BE SLIM BUT MUSCULAR

– being super-fit helps. Don't worry if you're not fit at the start of basic training. You will be by the end.

III. HAVE EXCELLENT VISION...

IV. Be able to read and write

If you're holding this, you can probably read, but how good's your lettering? Army life's not all sword-slashing, you know – there's some pen-pushing too.

V. Be a Roman citizen

You'll need proof – and a home-made toga from an old bedsheet isn't enough.

DO YOU MAKE THE GRADE?

Think you'll satisfy the entrance board? Then there's only an interview and medical to pass before you're in. But there are other qualities not mentioned on recruitment posters that could prove useful – see the quiz overleaf.

CAMP CHARACTER: A QUIZ

Study the parchment below and then answer the questions to see if you've got what it takes to be a Roman soldier.

QUALITIES
PATRIOTIC, LOYAL,
NOBLE, JUST,
COURAGEOUS,
GODS-FEARING, SERIOUS,
DISCIPLINED

I. Your twin brother turns against Rome: would you kill him?

II. You've made a bad mistake and brought shame upon your family: would you kill yourself?

III. You've been fighting a war for five years. Finally, you win. Do you make friends with the defeated army?

IV. Your commander gives what you think is a ludicrous order which will lead to certain death. Do you obey him instantly?

V. You're defending a bridge against an entire army. When it is finally destroyed, could you then jump into the river, fully armed and swim back to Rome?

If you answered "YES!" to all five questions, what are you waiting for? Find someone already serving to recommend you and join up today. You'll swear a simple oath of allegiance and the next 25 years of your life belong to the army. But where do you fit in?

ARMY ORGANIZATION

Where are you? At the bottom. You and seven other soldiers make up a contubernium, the smallest unit in the Roman Army. The largest is a legion with 5,120 soldiers. Think of contubernia* as bricks building the army. However many men there are in total, they all start out in groups of eight.

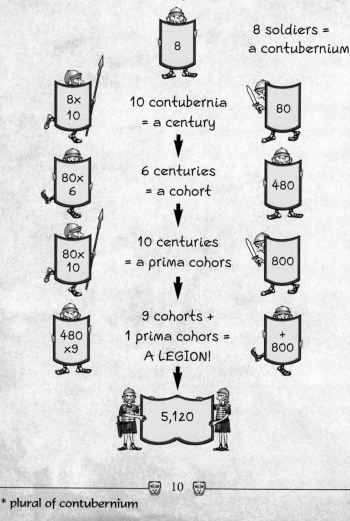

8 soldiers = a contubernium

10 contubernia = a century

6 centuries = a cohort

10 centuries = a prima cohors

9 cohorts + 1 prima cohors = A LEGION!

8

8× 10

80

80× 6

480

80× 10

800

480 ×9

+ 800

5,120

* plural of contubernium

PEOPLE AROUND CAMP

Fellow recruits stand out: they're exhausted and sweating, like you. But in case other uniforms are confusing, here's a spotter's guide to...

WHO'S SHOUTING AT ME NOW?

No. I, The Legate: commands the legion, always a senator, and hand-picked by the emperor himself. Unless you're spectacularly good (or bad), your paths won't cross.

Legate

No. II, Tribunes: six officers, led by a Senior Tribune – the legate's right-hand man. The other five are equestrian tribunes, in charge of paperwork and junior to the praefectus castrorum (below).

Senior Tribune

No. III, The Praefectus Castrorum: third in command and in charge of building camps when the army's on the move.

The P.C.

No. IV, The Primus Pilus: the most senior centurion around camp, he's the chief of the five senior centurions who command the prima cohors. He's also the most senior officer likely to get involved in any fighting. So give him respect.

Primus Pilus

No. V, The Centurion: in charge of a century and your immediate boss. Just pray you don't get landed with the infamous "Bring me another!" – so-called because he beats recruits until his cane snaps, when he cries (you guessed it), "Bring me another!"

Centurion

No. VI, The Optio: the centurion's second-in-command. Keep in with him. He'll report your every move to his boss.

Optio

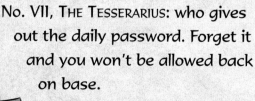

No. VII, The Tesserarius: who gives out the daily password. Forget it and you won't be allowed back on base.

Tesserarius

No. VIII, The Legionary: another name for an ordinary footsoldier – in other words: YOU!

Humble legionary

No. IX, The Auxiliaries: non-citizens from the provinces, grouped into cohorts of 500 to 1,000 men. They earn less than legionaries and get less training – but act as messengers and scouts, as well as fighters.

Auxiliaries on the battlefield fight in loose formation.

Auxiliary

Cavalry soldier

No. X, The Cavalry Soldier: on horseback and in the minority. Traditionally from the aristocracy (since connections and money were vital), but now drawn from the wider empire.

Two men hard to miss are the standard bearers, who carry troops' various emblems into battle.

AQUILIFER: bears the legion's standard, topped with the noble Roman eagle (aquila).

If the standard is lost in battle, your entire legion will be in disgrace (and serious trouble).

Aquilifer

Signifer

SIGNIFER: seen here carrying the standard of a maniple, or pair of centuries. (Maniple means "handful" hence the hand.) He's also in charge of the burial club. Pay up weekly and you're sure of a decent funeral.

Watch out for the pointed tips: they're sharp.

CORNICEN: the horn blower who helps you march in time. He also plays musical orders, such as "Eat!" If you don't want to starve (and to avoid a beating), pick the tunes up early on.

Cornicen

HANGERS ON

Soldiers are only some of the hundreds of people involved in keeping the army marching. Just because not all of the following fight, doesn't mean they're any less crucial. (Well, yes it does, but don't say that to their faces. You might need them one day.)

CLERK

In charge of admin, the camp's Official Penpusher

PRIEST (OR SEER)

In dire straits, praying may be all you have left.

DOCTOR

If things get this far, you'll just have to grin and 'bare' it.

SURVEYOR

The man who plans forts and camps.

(It's not that hard a job, since all forts and camps follow a similar layout.)

THE OPPOSITION

That's it for the guys on your side, but who might you be facing? Before you go on to read about the joys of basic training, here's a spotter's guide to...

THE BARBARIAN ENEMIES OF ROME

I. GERM-RIDDEN GERMANICS

Long, unwieldy sword

Flat shield

No protective clothing

* farmers and herders
* small groups of warriors serve a chief
* their land is handy for Gallia (north-west Europe) and full of iron
* to wind them up, grab their women and cattle

Chainmail tunic

Deadly spear

II. DEADLY DACIANS

* large army, equipped with war machines
* warriors trained in our fighting techniques by Roman fugitives, who are given a haven in Dacia

III. Gallumphing Gauls...

* less war-like than
Germanics
* VERY superstitious
* rely on priests called
Druids to help them
win battles

Vulnerable
bare
feet

Beats sword
against shield

...and Cold Celts

* very tall with shaggy,
bleached hair
* often fight naked,
making weird, harsh
shouts to unnerve
opponents
* cut off the heads of
victims and nail them
above their doors

IV. Parthian Pranksters

* the trickiest, most
dangerous enemy
* horse-archers fire
hundreds of arrows, while
moving so they can't be hit
* will flee and then round
on pursuers

CHAPTER II

LIFE OF A RAW RECRUIT

Yₒou'll soon know most people around camp, at least by sight. But you'll get to know the seven soldiers in your contubernium better than brothers. The most experienced one of you will be boss and, just so you don't forget, your contubernium will take his name.

BASIC TRAINING

Basic Training: for the first four months, you'll eat, sleep and breathe nothing else. New recruits are out twice a day – in wind, rain, hail or fog – perfecting battle drills, handling weapons and getting fit.

Just singin'
and marchin'
in the rain...

The eventual aim is for you all to react as one almost before the centurion barks his order. Remember: the army fights as a single unit.

**EVERY SOLDIER
MUST KNOW**

**I. WHAT TO DO
II. WHEN TO DO IT**

ALL TOGETHER NOW!

Acting in unison is probably one of the hardest things you'll have to master. But don't worry. An ingenious exercise has been devised which combines working as one with keeping fit: the ROUTE MARCH.

Take earplugs on marches.

Tone-deaf cats sound more tuneful.

On a normal route march, you'll cover 20 Roman miles (that's almost 30 kms and just over 18 miles) in five hours. But if your centurion is having a bad day – and he usually is – he could make you march 24 Roman miles (35.5 kms; 22 miles) in the same time.

You'll be sent on a route march about once every ten days. Singing rhythmic songs with fellow marchers can help you keep in step. (They're too rude to print here but you'll pick them up quickly enough.)

WHOLE KIT & KABOODLE

What makes a route march so bad is that you carry everything you'd take if you were moving camp. In fact, you often march

somewhere, set up camp and take it straight down again. This isn't because your centurion can't make up his mind but so you get used to putting up tents in a flash. (See pages 56-58.)

IN THE BAG

The combination of pack plus weapons can weigh over 30kgs (70lbs). Imagine carrying a large dog on your back for five miles.

As we say in the army: weight training? Who needs it?

BLOODLESS BATTLES: THE DRILL

When you're not marching or recovering on your bunk, you'll be on the parade ground working on drills and fake fights to learn how to handle weapons. You'll start with fake weapons: wooden swords and wicker shields, twice as heavy as the real thing, to build up strength.

If that sounds easy, try thrusting a heavy sword at a 1.8m (6ft) high wooden post. When you've cracked that, run up first.

You'll also be jumping forward, back, side to side, up and down... You may feel more like an acrobat than a soldier, but these moves all help to develop three vital fighting qualities:

I. Strength   II. Stamina   III. Agility

MARCHING ORDERS

In training and battle, centurions constantly bark instructions at you. The sort of commands you're likely to hear are listed below. Learn 'em or weep:

AD SIGNA (Fall in)
INTENTE! (Atten-tion!)
LAXATE (Stand at ease)

PROCEDITE (Forward march)
DEXTRORSUM VERTITE (Right turn)
SINISTRORSUM VERTITE (Left turn)
RETRORSUM VERTITE (About turn)
CONSISTITE (Halt)

SALUTATE (Salute)
PILA IN TERRAM (Put javelin in ground)
PILA SUMITE (Pick up javelin)
GLADIOS STRINGITE (Draw swords)
GLADIOS RECONDITE (Sheath swords)
SCUTA TOLLITE (Raise shields)
SCUTA DEMITTITE (Lower shields)

ITER ACCELERATE (Speed up)
ITER TARDATE (Slow down)
EXPECTATE... (Wait for it...)
AB SIGNIS DISCEDITE! (Dismiss!)

Altar to Jupiter (king of the gods) – every parade ground has one.
"On guard!"
Marching as one: keep in step or you'll be cleaning latrines all week.
Your training's at stake – it's a wooden practice column which can't fight back.

TRAINING
TREADMILL

Of course you might spend 25 years' service without seeing any battle action at all. You may even stay in the same garrison (army base) for your entire career.

Halt! Who goes zzzz...

You might ask:

If I'll never fight, why's the training so tough?

Answer:
Just in case. You must always be ready – you could be needed at any moment.

Besides, as every centurion knows, the only way to get an instant response – not to mention unquestioning obedience – is through harsh training.

No centurion is ever without his cane, worn down from continually beating legionaries. Which brings us to :

DISCIPLINE

THE ROMAN ARMY'S TOP FIVE PUNISHMENTS

In fifth place it's those:

(V) BEATINGS (V)

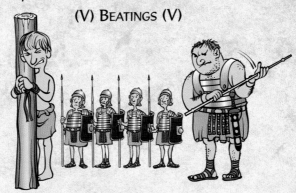

In fourth place, this will have you exhausted:

(IV) EXTRA FATIGUES (IV)

Coming in at number
three – and handy for
dieters – is:

(III) GOING WITHOUT (III)
RATIONS

Second, for theft or desertion (and getting more drastic) is:

(II) BEING BEATEN TO DEATH (II)

But none can topple the worst one of all. Yes, at number one, for cowardice, comes:

(I) DECIMATION (I)

Are you feeling lucky?

Get stuck in a cohort where someone runs away in battle and ten percent of the cohort has had it. Back at camp, lots are drawn and one out of every ten men is executed.

Even without actual wrong-doing, you'll need to keep up high standards to please your centurion. And they're arbitrary creatures. If one takes a dislike to you, you'd better make a speedy sacrifice to Mars, god of War...

PLEASING THE BOSS

Or try bribery. All officers accept bribes, usually from men hoping to escape unpleasant duties. The good news is you will receive a regular wage, so bribes can come out of this.

A vital move: the back-hander.

 # PAY AND CONDITIONS

As a legionary, you'll get a basic 300 denarii a year (far better than a craftsman). Auxiliaries get slightly less; cavalrymen slightly more. But, as you go up the ranks, so does your pay.

A junior officer, such as a tesserarius, has pay and a half. A senior officer, like a signifer, is on double pay. Centurions are on 4,500 denarii – before bribes – and the primus pilus has a whopping 18,000.

Don't think the army is a "Get rich quick" option. While food and clothes are organized by the army, you'll have to pay for them.

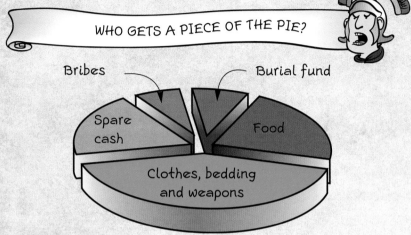

WHO GETS A PIECE OF THE PIE?

Bribes

Burial fund

Spare cash

Food

Clothes, bedding and weapons

FREE & SINGLE...

But what's left is all yours. There's a ban on soldiers marrying. If you were married already, the marriage was annulled when you enlisted – which you might want to tell your wife.

(Actually many soldiers keep families in civilian quarters outside the forts. The state just pretends they don't exist.)

PROMOTION & PATRONAGE

After a few years, if you want a promotion you'll need an influential relative (a patron). Ask him to write a letter saying how wonderful you are and you'll shoot up the career ladder on greased boots. You could try to impress your boss with a bold battle move instead (not so easy if there's no war and you're simply on guard duty).

Sucking up (or dusting down)

KEEP IT IN THE FAMILY

On the whole, promotion is gradual and rises to higher ranks take generations to happen.

Me, a legate

My son, the emperor?!

Great-granddad, a humble legionary

Dad, a primus pilus

CHAPTER III

READY FOR A FIGHT?

This chapter is where the real soldier stuff starts. From weapons to uniform, you'll find out what you get issued with and how to use them. What are you waiting for? Get to it!

WEAPONS OF ATTACK

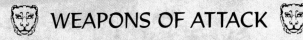

A quick question to begin. You're about to go into battle. Which of the following would you take as ATTACKING weapons?

I. PILUM (JAVELIN)

Wooden shaft (can be up to 120cms or 4ft long)

Sharp barbed point

Main stem of flexible iron (60-90cms or 2-3ft), long enough to go through shield and body

II. GLADIUS (SWORD)

Scabbard (cover)

Inside, the sword's blade (60cm or 18in long) is of the best-quality steel.

Long straps, so you can hang it from your shoulder

33

III. Pugio (dagger)

Rounded
at tip

Scabbard

The dagger's blade is made of iron or bronze.

IV. Scutum (shield)

Stands
120cms
(48in) high

Held together
by an iron rim

Bulge
known as
a "boss"

Curved to
provide
excellent
body
coverage
and deflect
missiles

70cms (28in)
wide

Made of solid layers of wood and leather,
shields can weigh up to 10kgs (22lbs).
So which would you take?
You might be surprised to learn that all four
can be used for attack, even the shield.

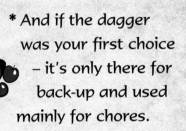

* If you thought a shield was only used to hide behind, check page 38. It's a useful weapon in its own right.

* And if the dagger was your first choice – it's only there for back-up and used mainly for chores.

Now for a look at them in more detail.

THREE THINGS TO KNOW ABOUT A PILUM

I. The iron rod goes in deeeeeeeeep.

II. Once it hits a shield it won't come out.

III. It bends on hitting the ground (so the enemy can't throw it back).

IMPORTANT THING ABOUT A GLADIUS

A legionary always wears it on his RIGHT
(even if he's left-handed). Think about it: in
battle you fight shoulder to shoulder, so
everyone must draw from the same side.

HOW TO DRAW YOUR SWORD

I. Grab the
handle, thumb
down.

II. Grasp
firmly and
pull out sword.

III. Once clear
of cover, point
up and out.

HOW TO USE YOUR SWORD

Slashing at an enemy might not hurt him badly enough if he's covered up. Besides, it leaves you open to attack under your slashing arm. Remember:

A THRUST BEATS A SLASH

Bring your sword back and...

...thrust it between your enemy's ribs.

HOW TO HOLD YOUR SHIELD

Hold on your left, with an overhand grip.

This grip makes your shield easier to carry.

Shield cover

The cover has straps so you can carry it on your back.

HOW TO USE YOUR SHIELD AS A WEAPON

The bulging "boss" in the middle of the shield is like having an iron fist, so you can:

PUNCH THEN STAB

When the enemy is near, smash the boss into him and follow up with a swift sword thrust.

UNIFORM

So much for weaponry. What about combat gear?

Well, first is the tunic. This is made from linen or wool, depending on where you're stationed and how hot – or cold – it gets.

Short sleeves

Embarrassingly short skirt

Of course, a tunic gives no protection at all, so over that you'll wear a mail vest, with leather pads on the shoulders. The alternative is a lorica segmentata, a metal breastplate held together by leather strips.

Mail vest

Lorica Segmentata

Leather pad

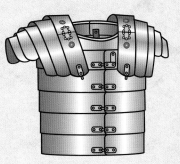

Overlapping iron strips give better protection.

Underneath are bracae, or wool leggings, for the cold. Leg guards, known as greaves, would be useful too, but they're only for officers (to show rank).

Bracae (can itch)

Metal greaves

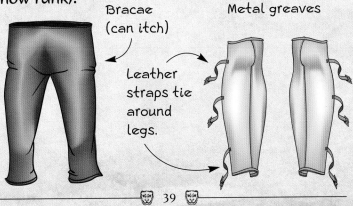

Leather straps tie around legs.

Then there's the helmet,
not entirely failsafe with large
parts left uncovered. And it's
heavy. (Imagine wearing a fat
frozen chicken on your head.)

Leather strings tie
under chin.

Hinged guards protect cheeks.

Inside fittings are attached
with rivets, so helmets are
lined with wool or linen
padding. This quickly gets
worn from dirt and sweat,
so replace it regularly.

Going from top to toe, on your feet
you'll wear sandals, aka caligae.
They're hard-wearing enough for
marches, but you only get
three pairs a year, so look
after them.

They're designed not
to rub, but grease
new pairs with oil.

The soles are studded with
hobnails for rough terrain
and gripping on grass.

Don't worry if you're posted somewhere cold and damp. For murky, miserable Britannia, you'll get a pair of boots like these.

For travel and cold nights on guard duty, you'll get a wool cloak (which can double as a blanket). You also get a scarf so your uniform doesn't rub your neck.

Finally, you'll wear a cingulum militare, a belt with studded leather strips hanging down the front. It won't give extra protection, but it does jingle as you walk, so people know you're coming and get out of the way.

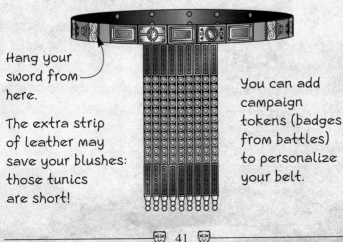

Hang your sword from here.

The extra strip of leather may save your blushes: those tunics are short!

You can add campaign tokens (badges from battles) to personalize your belt.

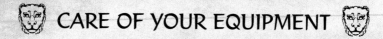

A simple sum:

I bent pilum + II sloppy sandals
= I bad soldier

Your uniform doesn't have to gleam on parade (unless the emperor's around), but it must protect you in battle. Metal rusts quickly, especially in damp countries, so:

KEEP IT WELL GREASED!

Keep all leather well-greased too: not only will it last longer, it will also be more flexible. Olive oil or animal fat – with plenty of elbow grease – should do the trick.

To shift rust, make a paste of sand and oil or fat and rub in well.

CHAPTER IV

LET BATTLE COMMENCE!

Roman soldiers are renowned for two things: their ferocity in battle and their absolute refusal to surrender. But, before the battle even starts, there are various tricks you can use to knock the enemy off-balance.

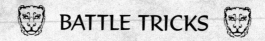

BATTLE TRICKS

I. KEEP THE SUN AT YOUR BACK

Any glare
will blind the
enemy.

II. CHECK THE WIND DIRECTION

If it's blowing away from you, dust will fly
into the enemy's faces, causing coughing,
confusion and chaos. Missiles go further too.

III. GRAB A HEIGHT ADVANTAGE

If there's a hill,
make sure you're
on top.

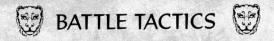 BATTLE TACTICS

For use as the fight begins:

I. THROW THEM BEFORE THEY THROW YOU

To unnerve the enemy
from the start, advance
slowly and in
ABSOLUTE
SILENCE.

When your massed ranks are about 15m
(50ft) away, hurl your pila* and charge forward
with swords drawn, screaming a battle cry as
you go.

II. STICK TOGETHER

Give the enemy no chance to break through
your ranks and, if they don't run from your
terrifying charge, try hand-to-hand combat.

* plural of pilum

III. USE BATTLE FORMATIONS

THE SAW: keeps a unit immediately behind the front line, which can move to block any holes.

Front line

Hole in front line

Moving in to block the hole

THE WEDGE:

Enemy ranks

Breaking through the enemy ranks

Form a triangle, with one soldier at the tip. Thrust into the enemy, then spread out.

This neat move gives the enemy no room to swing their long and, let's face it, frankly unwieldy swords.

The Orb (a circle):

a defensive position and the last resort. Only form this if completely outnumbered.

It's a fight you'll lose – but you'll go down fighting.

The Testudo (or Tortoise):

Form a rectangle, holding your shields over your heads, or before you if you're at the front. This creates an almost impenetrable barrier and is especially useful in a siege (see pages 52-53).

The tortoise is so strong, a cart could be driven over the top.

The Skirmish: simply a widely spaced line-up,

giving you more room to fight – though it does also give the enemy more chance to penetrate.

IV. GET IN BATTLE ORDER

Everyone has a set place to stand when they line up for battle, carefully designed so weaker troops can be supported by stronger ones. One possible battle line-up is shown below.

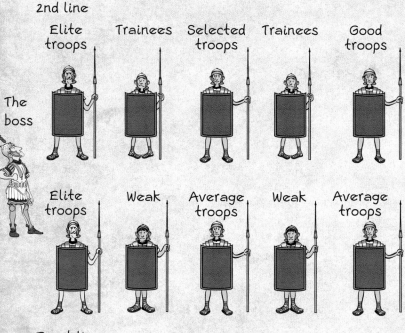

2nd line

Elite troops   Trainees   Selected troops   Trainees   Good troops

The boss

Elite troops   Weak   Average troops   Weak   Average troops

Front line

OMENS

Of course, none of the above is any use if the gods aren't on your side. Your commander should check for encouraging signs before he gives the order to fight. Some of the signs to look out for are shown opposite.

Yes!!

* feeding sacred hens
(if they eat, attack)

* checking entrails
(leave this to
the seer)

* seeing an eagle
in the sky (could
be good, could
be bad)

You can help with
sacrifices and sending
up the odd prayer
to Mars.

VICTORY PROCESSION

Standard bearers followed by centurions

Last (and least), you

The Emperor (daubed in red to show he is almost a god)

Remember: you're only a man!

A servant stands behind the Emperor, to ensure he doesn't get big-headed.

A tradition loved by emperors and sportsmen alike, after a triumphant battle comes the glorious parade. This is your chance to enjoy fifteen minutes of fame, drinking in the cheers of the adoring crowd. Feel free to hurl the odd insult at your Emperor, as he acknowledges the waving crowd. It's thought to bring good luck.

Cheering crowd (which doesn't hurl insults, on pain of death)

Twelve men known as lictors carry rods (symbols of authority)

Captured loot

Prisoners of war (who'll be sold as slaves or killed)

Animals for sacrifice

Senators and other important politicians – who don't fight but are happy to share the glory – grab the lead.

 SIEGES

Of course, you won't always face your enemy on the battlefield. Sometimes they hole up in town and refuse to leave. Luckily, starving them out is a thing of the past, thanks to useful technology invented by the Ancient Greeks.

BATTERING RAM: a simple but effective way to break through walls, inside there's a tree trunk suspended from ropes.

"SCORPION" CATAPULT: used to fire bolts and deadly accurate.

MECHANICAL CROSSBOW: large and stationary but can fire two bolts at once.

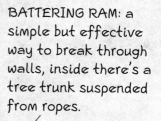

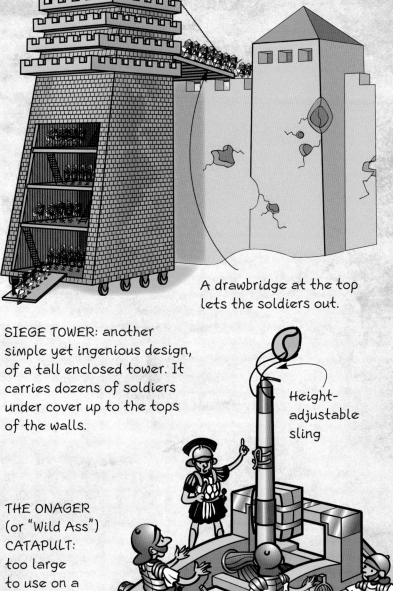

A drawbridge at the top lets the soldiers out.

SIEGE TOWER: another simple yet ingenious design, of a tall enclosed tower. It carries dozens of soldiers under cover up to the tops of the walls.

Height-adjustable sling

THE ONAGER (or "Wild Ass") CATAPULT: too large to use on a battlefield, this throws massive rocks over 300m (900ft).

DONE ANY CARPENTRY?

...because before you can fire the siege engines, you have to build them. Do this away from the city to be safe from enemy fire.

HOW LOW (DOWN & DIRTY) CAN YOU GO?

Try screwing up the enemy by:

i) firing the severed heads of spies over the walls; and

ii) building a second ditch and wall around existing ones. This not only stops help from reaching the city, it reminds the rebels they're trapped.

AFTERMATH

Once you've broken through, it's all over bar the shouting (massacring and looting). Your commanders will have given the besieged every chance to surrender before the attack. If they held out at the first hit of the ram: GIVE NO MERCY! You're not simply punishing them, you're warning other cities not to hold out too.

CHAPTER V

CAMPS, FORTS AND HADRIAN'S WALL

With such a vast empire to defend, you could be sent anywhere from Syria (hot) to Britannia (not). But you'll soon feel at home because all camps and forts are built in a similar pattern.

SETTING UP CAMP

Camps have two purposes:
    (I) to keep you safe,
    (II) to impress the enemy. Seeing an entire tent village go up in next to no time is enough to unnerve anyone. It helps that everything is always in the same place.

A centurion's tent

Contubernium's tent

Supper break

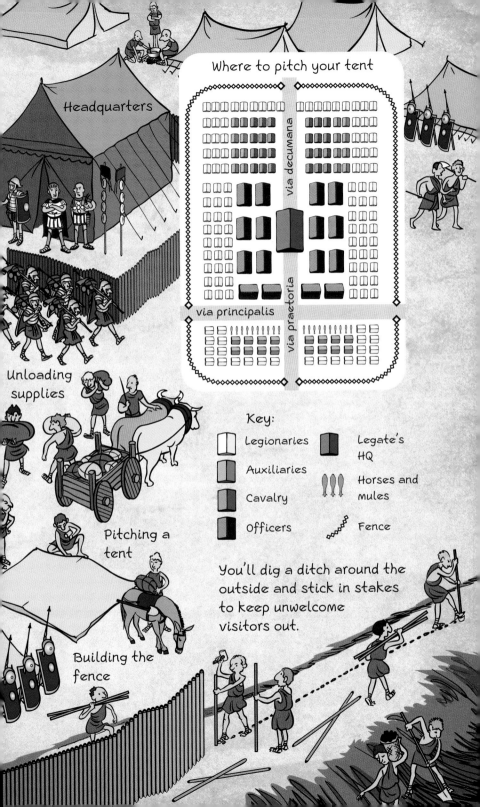

Headquarters

Where to pitch your tent

via decumana

via principalis

via praetoria

Unloading supplies

Key:

Legionaries

Auxiliaries

Cavalry

Officers

Legate's HQ

Horses and mules

Fence

Pitching a tent

You'll dig a ditch around the outside and stick in stakes to keep unwelcome visitors out.

Building the fence

The tents are loaded on baggage carts or mules. You'll carry everything else. To make sure you don't leave anything behind, check the list below.

PACK CHECKLIST
- UNIFORM ☐
- WEAPONS ☐
- POTS AND PANS ☐
- FOOD RATION ☐
- BEDDING ☐
- PERSONAL BELONGINGS ☐
- TWO STAKES FOR FENCE ☐

FRONTIER FORTS

When you're not on the move, you'll live in a permanent base on the edge of the empire. Forts pretty much follow the layout of camps, though with plenty of added extras, such as stables, foodstores, workshops, latrines, a bath house, bakery and hospital.

Plan of a fort for 800 men

Key:

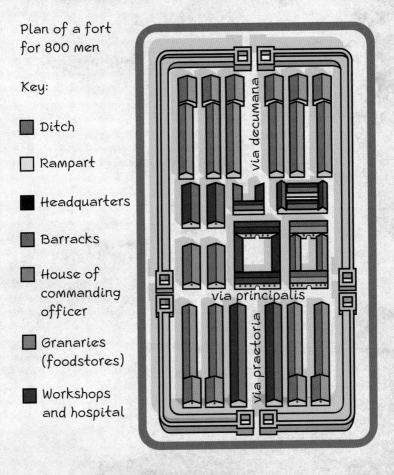

■ Ditch

□ Rampart

■ Headquarters

■ Barracks

■ House of commanding officer

■ Granaries (foodstores)

■ Workshops and hospital

via decumana

via principalis

via praetoria

A QUICK TOUR INSIDE A FORT: THE ARMY HQ

The headquarters, or principia, is the main office and bank for the camp. The most precious things are housed here: the legion's standard, a bust of the emperor – and your wages.

Cross hall (or basilica) where you'll gather for orders

Records room

Chapel (with permanent guard)

Notices are pinned on the other side of this wall. Keep an eye out for important announcements, such as inspections.

THE GRANARY (STOREHOUSE)

You won't go hungry – granaries are kept full of grain, huge joints of meat and plenty of vegetables to build up energy for your marches.

Unloading sacks of grain

A ROOM IN A BATH HOUSE

You can be sure every fort will have comfortable baths where you can take a dip and relax with friends.

THE COMMANDER'S HOUSE

While you're squashed in tiny barracks, your commanding officer, together with his wife and family (he gets to keep his), can really spread out. In fact, most commanders' houses take up easily a tenth of any fort. This is his official residence though, so it's also used to host banquets and house visiting VIPs.

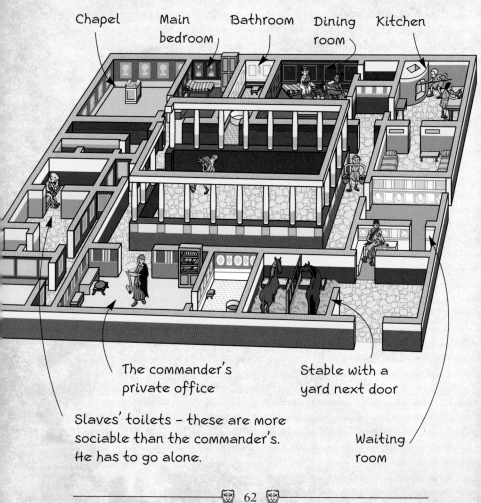

Chapel
Main bedroom
Bathroom
Dining room
Kitchen

The commander's private office

Stable with a yard next door

Slaves' toilets – these are more sociable than the commander's. He has to go alone.

Waiting room

Your quarters are much more basic but at least they won't let in rain (unlike tents). Each contubernium shares a pair of rooms in one of the long, narrow barrack blocks.

Weapons

Smelly feet

The biggest problem is snoring. If you don't have earplugs, balls of candle wax are almost as good.

Sleeping quarters are in the back room, with the weapons store in front. You'll have a small brazier for heating, if you've been posted somewhere cold, but that's it.

FORT LIFE

You won't get to spend much time in your sleeping quarters anyway. From the moment the bugle blows at dawn, you'll be up and hard at work. The question is:

ARE YOU A MILES OR AN IMMUNIS?

As a new recruit you'll probably be a miles and get the worst tasks: guard duty (boring) or cleaning – the principia, the bathhouse or the latrines (enough said).

Without a trade, you'll be stuck scrubbing toilets.

There's a chance you may go on road patrol or do police work, but your safest bet is to get a trade or skill as soon as possible. As a skilled immunis, you'll escape the dirty jobs and instead could be a fighting butcher, blacksmith, engineer, clerk or vet.

WHAT'S UP DOC?

If you don't faint at the sight of blood (and if you do, why are you in the army?), you could always be an army doctor. Army hospitals are where Roman medicine is learned. It's not hard, since treatment is basic (though effective).

You'll mostly be setting broken bones or hacking off limbs if they're too far gone to save. But there's also a range of medicines at your disposal. If all else fails, simply remind your patient his health is in the hands of the gods.

A good supply of wine – it's the only anaesthetic

Remember! Garlic each day keeps illness at bay.

An apprentice learning his trade

ALL ROADS LEAD TO ROME...

...and most were built by the army. For a life in the open air, train as an engineer, stone mason or carpenter. The army always has some building project on the go.

Roads, especially, are essential for an army on the move, not to mention messengers and trade. Yet parts of the empire are so backward, they hardly have any. (As for aqueducts carrying clean water – you can only assume the barbarians never wash.)

Stuck on road-building duty, you'll spend all day breaking up rocks or digging foundations.

Be warned: you'll have to build a mile (1,000 paces) every three days.

Roads are built up in layers, on a bank between two ditches.

Shifting slabs into place

When your legion reaches a river, you'll be building the bridge across it. There's a choice of two. Pontoon bridges, made of wood and resting on barges, can go up in days. If time isn't an issue, you'll be building in solid stone.

BUILD YOUR OWN FRONTIER

In fact, you could spend quite a lot of your time building things. Emperor Hadrian has put a stop to expansion, deciding the empire's quite big enough. But he wants all wooden forts to be rebuilt in stone, plus walls, fences and ditches built along the frontiers.

A milecastle (fortified gateway) on Hadrian's Wall

Milecastles are built along the wall every Roman mile.

Changing the guard

Keeping watch

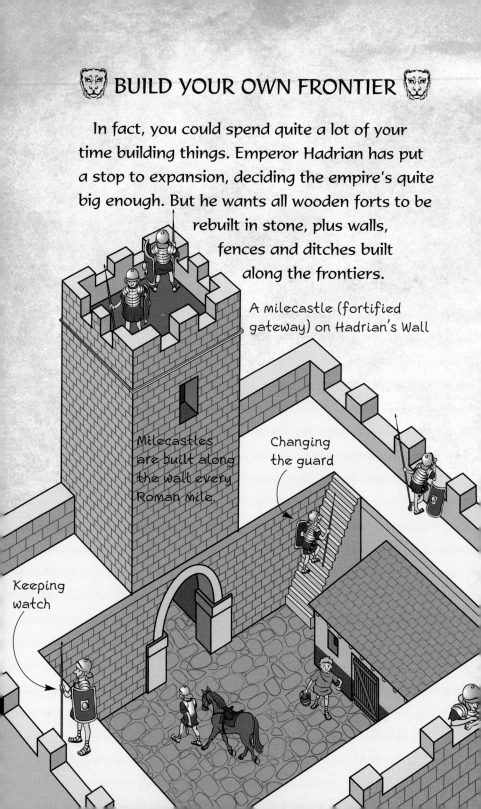

LIVING ON THE EDGE

Browsing in the market

Out with an unofficial girlfriend

Cloth for family back home

Most forts along the edges of the empire are well established – so settled, that towns have grown up around them. And there's no shortage of traders, keen to talk you out of your wages.

A town on the doorstep is especially useful when it comes to time off. You can spend a traditional day out, shouting yourself hoarse at a gladiator fight or the races. Or borrow a horse and head to the country for a hunt.

Being a chariot rider can be as dangerous as soldiering.

What you can hunt depends on where you're posted. Expect to chase bears or deer in a northern province – or leopards, lions and wild boar in Africa.

Here's your chance to get close to animals you may only have seen at the Colosseum.

But if that's too much action, try a show at the local playhouse, where you're guaranteed fake blood and a laugh.

ARE YOU BEING SENT OVERSEAS?

Don't panic if you're posted a long way from home. Just read these useful tips to make your stay more fun.

* Find out about the native gods and include them in your prayers and sacrifices just in case. You don't want to start offending local deities.

* Share Roman customs, such as roads and bathing, with the natives, but don't be closed off to their traditions. OK, some paint themselves before battle. War paint may suit you.

* As for the weather, all you need remember is: Africa's hotter, Britannia's wetter.

* Get friendly with a messenger and arrange for relatives to send you the occasional package from home. There are bound to be several things you miss.

* Be prepared to learn the local language. You may be here for the next 25 years.

* Find out which natives are friendly – and which ones aren't (mostly the ones on the wrong side of the frontier).

CHAPTER VI

HANDY REFERENCE

Annual Legionaries
vs Centurions Quiz

For all those situations where you're put on the spot by an officer with a knack for asking tricky questions, whip out this section. Covering army history and tactics, it finishes with a map of the empire – so you can see where the bad guys are coming from.

A HISTORY OF THE ARMY
(with the boring bits left out)

The Roman Army's strength is largely thanks to the sheer number of battles it fights. Here are a few highlights, beginning in the early republic when there was hardly an army at all.

c.510BC on: Soldiers are property owners (usually farmers). Wars are near Rome and brief.

c.396BC: Soldiers are paid for the first time.

340BC: Wars move away from Rome, which means the farmer-soldiers have to leave their farms for longer. The soldiers are still handier with a hoe than a sword. Only the rich citizens can afford weapons and protective clothes.

BASICALLY, THE ARMY'S A RABBLE

387BC: Gauls from northern Europe attack and invade Rome.

350BC: The army tries to pull itself together.

343-290BC: The Samnites, a tribe from central Italy, decide Rome is getting too strong and three wars with them follow. Rome also defeats an alliance of Latin cities.

280-275BC: The Pyrrhic Wars – battles with an army led by King Pyrrhus of northern Greece over a Greek city in Italy.

264BC on: The famous Punic Wars with the city of Carthage on the North African coast begin.

264-241BC: 1st Punic War means building a navy.

THE ARMY LEARNS THE ART OF FIGHTING AT SEA

218-201BC: 2nd Punic War, started by Hannibal, a Carthaginian general governing the Carthaginian territory of Spain. Hannibal leads an army of 35,000 men and 37 elephants over the Alps. Taken by surprise, the Roman army suffers a crushing defeat. Hannibal wins a lot of fights.

ROMAN GENERALS START COPYING HANNIBAL

Hannibal is finally defeated by Scipio, a Roman commander, in 202BC.

149-146BC: 3rd Punic War – Carthage destroyed.

107BC: Marius, a soldier and politician, becomes a Roman consul and introduces army reforms:

* Anyone can join
* All soldiers have the same weapons and training
* Troops carry their own equipment, so they can travel faster
* The Legions are organized into ten cohorts
* The Eagle becomes the only standard of the Roman legion

THE ARMY BECOMES WHAT IT IS TODAY

88BC: Sulla, Marius's former lieutenant, becomes consul and picks a fight with Mithridates, King of Asia Minor. Marius is given command of the army. Sulla is furious and marches on Rome.

88-66BC: Mithridates is equally cross. Three wars follow.

73-70BC: The slaves in Italy are crosser. The army is called in to quell their rebellion.

60BC: Two ex-consuls, Pompey and Crassus, form an alliance with newcomer Julius Caesar.

THE RISE OF CAESAR MEANS PLENTY OF BATTLES

58-50BC: Caesar conquers Gaul.

55 and 54BC: Caesar invades Britain.

54-3BC: Crassus invades Parthia – a big mistake, as he's defeated and killed.

49-45BC: Caesar and Pompey argue. Civil war breaks out.

44-42BC: Caesar is assassinated by Brutus and Cassius, leading to another civil war, this time beween them and the team of Mark Antony and Octavian, Caesar's adopted son.

42BC: Brutus and Cassius lose. Mark Antony and Octavian divide Roman territory into East and West. Mark Antony moves in with Cleopatra, Queen of Egypt. Tension grows between Octavian and Mark Antony.

31BC: The sea battle of Actium – Octavian defeats Mark Antony.

27BC: Augustus, formerly known as Octavian, becomes emperor, starting the Roman Empire.

BIRTH OF IMPERIAL ARMY; THE INVASIONS GO ON

43AD: Claudius launches invasion of Britain.

58-64AD: More wars with Parthia.

60AD: Britons, led by Boudicca, rebel and are defeated.

66-74AD: The Jews rebel but are only defeated after eight years of fighting and sieges.

68-69AD: Emperor Nero's death means civil war.

70sAD: Britons cause trouble.

86-106AD: On and off battles with the Dacians for twenty years, which the Romans finally win.

113-117AD: Buoyed up by victory, Emperor Trajan decides to fight the Parthians and expands the empire to its greatest extent.

117-138AD: Emperor Hadrian declares the empire is quite big enough and the invasions should stop. He begins a massive building scheme on the frontiers.

ARMY USED TO DEFEND EXISTING FRONTIERS

142-164AD: Antoninus Pius tries to expand into Scotland, building his own Wall, but it doesn't last.

162-180AD: The Parthians attack in the East and the Marcomanni, a German tribe, attack in the North. From now on, attacks on the empire will hardly ever stop.

193-197AD: Emperor Commodus's assassination means more civil wars.

235AD on: Invasions and raids into the empire go on. Whenever an emperor dies (or is murdered), another leaps up to take his place.

BATTLE PLAN

As a rule, tactics are the concern of your commander, but it might help to have at least a vague idea of what's going on in his head. The diagrams below show a typical and popular battle plan.

Cavalry   Roman army   Cavalry

Enemy cavalry   Enemy   Enemy cavalry

I. The cavalry attacks the enemy's cavalry, while the front line of legionaries advances to break up the enemy front line.

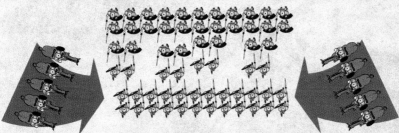

II. The second line moves in, to fill any gaps and the cavalry returns to attack from the rear.

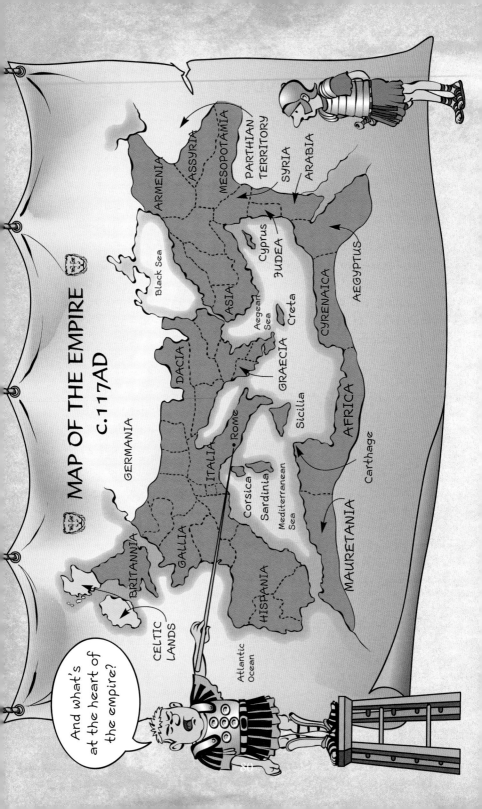

INDEX